HARLEM NIGHTS and
FOOTSTEP BLUES

ISBN: 0997172606

ISBN 13: 978-0-9971726-0-7

HARLEM NIGHTS and FOOTSTEP BLUES

JULIUS JAMAAL MCLEAN

Contents

Acknowledgments

I thank God for the opportunity that I've been given in this world to create meaningful work. I also would like to thank all of my family, friends, supporters, and everyone who has listened to or read and enjoyed anything that I've ever written. Many of those individuals have left an indelible impact on my life and, as a result, have influenced and inspired the eclectic mix of work contained in this collection. I wouldn't have been able to create everything in the way that I have without their impact. My mother has always been an example of how to pursue a desire fervently through her diligence and dedication. I'm grateful to have her as an example that has prepared me in the pursuit of all my endeavors in life. I have to thank my sister Andrea and my aunt Carol for their unwavering support. My grandmother Nellie has been a constant source of inspiration, both while living and even now after her passing. She still serves as a shining example of how a full life should be lived. My cousin Clint has been a mental sparring partner for me, and he has proved to be a peer who has inspired me to increase my level of performance in everything, including the process of writing this collection. My high-school teacher Ms. Jones challenged me as a writer more than anyone ever has. She also made me believe in my ability to write, and for that I thank her. Two Nupes, Kareem and Omari, have helped me cultivate my ability to think and write critically and creatively. Their mentorship has been instrumental in my personal and artistic growth. Langston Hughes has been the mentor whom I've never met, and his influence can be found throughout my work. I have to thank Justin Reed for his wonderful cover art, which is visually reflective of everything that this collection represents. I'm very appreciative of his creative vision. Finally, I would like to thank my nephews and little cousins because they are constantly showing me and reminding me of the power of youth, enthusiasm, and every other important thing that I've forgotten as I've progressed through life.

SEEDS

A Baby's Eyes

What lives within a baby's eyes?
Wonder? Confusion? Surprise?

Twinkling stars of essence—
Uncompromised.

Those bright little eyes—
Searching the skies—
Surfing on imaginative
Boards fueled by Power Cosmic.

What lives within a baby's eyes?
Things that we no longer realize
Are dear.

A baby's eyes are clear.
A baby's eyes don't veer
Away from the truth.
A baby's eyes are pure—
Full of youth
And unbridled curiosity.
A baby's eyes contain a flame
That becomes dormant in older age,
A flame that we should rekindle again.
The child is the father of man
Who once understood what
Man must understand again,
After the degenerative
Loss of his natural intuitiveness.

A baby's eyes are uninfluenced
By society's environmental pollutants.

A baby's eyes contain the blueprint
For achieving unparalleled bliss.
A baby's eyes should be prized
As a symbol of all that we should strive
To be.
A baby's eyes inspire me
T…
To…
To b…
To be.

Jumpman

What is it in the symbol

That makes all the competition tremble?

Is it the peak that the legs resemble

As they stretch apart so graceful and nimble?

Or how Isaac Newton is vehemently defied,

Because on it the laws of gravity cannot be applied?

How it challenges the notion that man can't fly

And dares us all to touch the sky?

Its flight declares "impossible" a lie!

Its existence reminds us to continually try!

Namekian Dragonballs

When I was a child,
I had the same smile,
And my mind was filled
With thoughts
Of Namekian Dragonballs
And Rock Bottom pinfalls.
When I'd withdraw
From those imaginary thoughts,
My mind would then drift
To a penthouse loft.
I knew that my wishes
Would be granted
By Porunga,
The Dragon of Dreams.
As the years passed,
I'd drift further
And further
On my Nimbus cloud.
And I had no doubt
That my wishes
Would be granted
By Porunga,
The Dragon of Dreams.

MUSES

Sanctuary

Peace comes under the night sky,
With Friday-night lights so bright.
Just me, the sky, the lights, her,
And thunderous words
In the language of blue concrete.
My heart bleeds
Out to the lazy streets,
Where cars pass ever so often,
An occasional audience
To witness my awesomeness
And this eternal bliss.
This is what I've missed!

After all my strivings for greatness,
I've come full circle to this:
The simplicity of what has always calmed me
And the realization that it is what I need.
It is as vital an instrument to my life as breath,
And whatever I am without it is surely death.
If I were stripped of all that makes me,
This would be what's left.
And somehow it left me,
Or, more accurately,
I left it to be on my own.
Shoulda been my first, but it's my last resort—
My Spirit Bomb of sorts.

Thoughts flood my mind,
Reminders of the times—
Times of sacrifices made for gains
That were in gallons of sweat paid—

Times of ignorant days
And innocent games played—
Times in which I was made.
This place should be my grave.
After all the things that have changed,
Back to those things I've come.
Just me, the sky, the lights, her,
And thunderous words
In the language of blue concrete.

Lost Love

She and I have grown too far apart,
Her presence erased from within my heart.
She and I can never be.
I'm married to a dream that isn't She.
She and I have history,
But She's slowly becoming a distant memory.
She and I were once We,
But now there's just Her and just Me.
She and I made love together.
I thought I would be with Her forever.
She and I once harmonized.
Now I long for what She felt like.
She and I shared starry nights;
We bathed together at twilight.
She and I were inseparable
Until I chose to let Her go.
She and I were destined to fail,
As I courted several other girls.
She and I, the fan we hit;
To Her alone I couldn't commit.
She groomed Me.
I failed She.
We will never be.

She

She's a beautiful abyss.

My eyes get stuck in her midst.

Her beauty is a labyrinth to get lost in.

The depths of her soul are a bottomless pit within.

Face, a sculpture chiseled to perfection—

Ventriloquist with her eyes—

Massage therapist with her thighs.

I wonder what deep within her soul lies.

Of her inner workings, I can only fantasize

Of a time in which my dream will be fully realized.

Until then I am constantly captivated

By this benchmark of pulchritude that God has created

For me and me alone.

My Jada Pinkett, my Nia Long—

With her is where I belong.

And without her I'd rather be alone,

Waiting atop my empty throne

For a queen who can do much more than hold her own

In this game of love and war that we play together—

Two separate souls searching for forever.

My Lucky Girl

Crumbling down the world
Comes, in the absence of my lucky girl.
Shell of my former self
I am, in the absence of my pearl.
The odds just ain't the same,
And now my luck no longer remains.
Unplayable becomes the game
In the absence of my lucky girl.
Maybe one day we'll reconcile,
Your love for me will grow
Fonder in your heart after a while,
And I'll stop thinking in clichéd tropes.
Maybe I've reached the end of the rope,
And lost is all hope
Of you and I eloped,
As the light at the end
Of the tunnel descends
To night's skin.
Perhaps this is the end,
And I'll know what it's like to win
Without you,
Because winning is
All that I can do,
Even when I lose.
In the absence of you,
I think that I'm falling in love
With the blues.
Reality is a lie
That I refuse to give in to.

Mother Nellie

Mother Nellie
Used to sit on the back pew
In the right corner,
And everyone who walked in knew
Her and adored her.
"Giving honor to God,"
She would say.
"Thanks for a healthy body."
And the church would say, "Amen."
And I would sit in the back
And pretend
To be awake.

She would say, "Smoochie"—
That's what she called me—
"Do you have any money
For offering?"
And then I'd grin
Because I knew
What would happen
Next—she would give me
A dollar for offering
And a dollar to spend
At the corner store,
Enough for a Donut Stick
And a Ritz.
I still remember way back when.

And when Mother Nellie's
Legs were no longer present
And her chair wheels spun,

Mother Nellie would roll in
And sit next to the back pew
In the right corner.
My cousin Ty
Was beside her,
And when it was time,
He would guide her
Back to the car.

And when Mother Nellie
Lay in her hospital bed,
I'm certain that in her head,
She envisioned herself smiling
And sitting on the back pew
In the right corner.
And to this day
I mourn her
As God's fallen soldier
Who lived her life as a warrior.
From grandson to grandmother,
I love her.

Conversations with Langston

Once in a while,
Our souls meet.
We sit down,
Discuss poetry, and eat.
I tell him how much
I admire his work,
And he tells me how
Proud he is that he birthed
Me from his dream,
The moment after
It did explode.
Not one word was ever spoken—
He tells me things from the words he wrote.
I understand him,
And he understands me.
He knows his legacy
Is safe with me.
I might be the only
One who can see
That on the island,
He sits happily
On fair sands
Under his dream-blossomed tree,
Watching me make waves
In the comfort of his work's shade.

Josephine

Could you be
The muse of my dreams,
My dear Josephine?
Through you,
My poetry
Is based on a true story.

To your body
Be the glory.
And may your essence
Be the inspiration for
A timeless allegory
Of beauty and art.

DESTINED TO FAIL

Clipped Wings

Clipped wings
And shattered dreams—
The prison cells have transformed
Men into lesser beings.
The men in my life
Have reached their twilight
Far too early.

Victims of political savagery—
Fathers, uncles, and cousins,
Absentee husbands,
Rendered absolutely powerless.
Some guilty, some innocent,
All victims nonetheless.
Reduced to household figureheads—
Unfit for the structure that society has built
And wearing the scarlet letter of their own guilt.

The prison industrial scissors
Have left their wings severed,
Without leaving a feather
To fly upward.
The prison industrial hammer
Has left their dreams shattered
Into a million broken promises
To self and caused all confidence
To melt until nothingness remains.
The prison industrial machine
Claims another victim to its regime
And another witness to its shame.
I've seen many men whom it has claimed

Go in and never come out the same.
I've lost many men in my life
To its impervious grip of vise.

Father

Got a phone call from my father
And didn't know what to say.
The void he left unfilled,
I filled it in my own way.

Got a phone call from my father;
He didn't know what to say.
I know he wishes he was there for me,
But it just didn't work that way.

Got a phone call from my father
And didn't feel a thing.
I didn't even look to blame him;
I'm nothing but a machine.

Machines don't have feelings.
Machines don't have fathers.
So why would I even bother
To feel anything?

Got a phone call from my father,
And I wish that I could feel something.
The void he left unfilled,
I filled it with nothing.

Machine

[100 1001]

[010 0000]

[100 0001][100 1101]

[010 0000]

[100 1111][100 1110][100 1100][101 1001]

[010 0000]

[100 0001]

[010 0000]

[100 1101][100 0001][100 0011][100 1000][100 1001][100 1110][100 0101]

[I]

[(space)]

[A][M]

[(space)]

[O][N][L][Y]

[(space)]

[A]

[(space)]

[M][A][C][H][I][N][E]

The Matrix

The Matrix is a baseless trap,
Marked by the loss of independent thought.
Its systematic dominion is an intricate diversion
That subverts our courage and inner purpose.
We are designed in a world that erases our identity
And preselects our divinities.
We are spoon-fed tragedies
By our handpicked majesties.

The Matrix is a veil of lies
That blinds our eyes.
It drains our minds
And steers our lives.
Our binary world of ones and zeros—
Villains and heroes,
Painted strokes of black and white,
With everything solely wrong or right—
Has given us everything short of life.

The Matrix was created by man
And yet persecutes its creator.
It annihilates humanity
Through ill-advised vanity.
Clever beasts ensnared
By the invention of nothingness,
Conceptualizing concepts,
And theorizing theories,
We've fallen so far from
The nature of nature.

The Matrix is a plague
That leaves society in a terminal stage
Of life.
It is contrived of contrivance,
An infinite loop of metaphorical
Nonsense posing as truth.
It's a beanstalk so giant
That we've forgotten the root.

The Matrix thrives on abstraction.
In it, perception
Is based on the assumption
Of the congruency of unequal things
That satiate our desire for understanding.
By discarding what is individual and actual,
We condense reality into a categorical
Conception of meaningful perceptions.

The Matrix is only a tool,
A necessary evil
Not necessarily to be taken literally.
It is vital to comprehension
But demands a fine line to be walked
Within our thoughts.
We must live both within
And outside of it,
Utilizing it, but realizing
That it is not real.
We're so lost in it,
But we must learn again to feel
And balance the contemporaneity
Of our Matrix and reality.

Programmed Obsolescence

Our structure is frail—
Destined to fail
By design.
We're confined
To the lines
That they've decided
We stay inside—
Not completely refined
Like the iPhone 5,
Because the iPhone 6 is not far behind.
It's a business,
And it's time we realized this.
Broken blacks
Are more profitable
Than those fully intact
To America's success.
Things we deem as impressive signs of progress
Are often means of progressive regression.

Bricks

Bloodstained bricks—
The land of the free
Was built with
Bloodstained bricks,
With fingerprints
From the hands
Of enslaved men,
And the spoils of genocide
Of indigenous men,
Natives to the land.

Bloodstained bricks—
The evidence of foul play
That cannot be washed away—
Suspended in a state
Of perpetual shame,
They paint over the bricks
But can't remove the stain.
The home of brave
Was built on pain.

Bloodstained bricks—
Each brick laid by undying lies,
Ignoring the pleas of crying eyes.
Long live the apparitions
Of brick builders forced into submission.
They haunt the dreams of politicians.
In history books, they're seldom mentioned.
Take heed the legend of the bloodstained bricks,
Full of life and full of death,
Built on lies and forged with sin.
This land was paved by martyred men.

The Atlanta Compromise

The Atlanta compromise
Still lingers
On the tips
Of the fingers
Of weak-minded
Black figures

That support accommodationism,
Watered down by patriotism,
And dismiss
Black nationalism
As radicalism
That interferes with the
Carlton Banks agenda.

Real coonery
Is buffoonery
From blacks who believe
That they're fighting the machine
By shuffling their feet
For a false sense of immunity.

Salute to the Tuskegee Machine
That planted the seed
Of doubt, which makes us deem
Ourselves unworthy
Of being noteworthy.

They want Marshawn and Sherman
In the closet
And an automaton

Up in the front posing
For the camera.

Deep down they believe
Our black skin has damned
Us. In God we trust
For better or worse.
It hurts
When I hear those ashamed
Of how the black mouth works.
It's the most beautiful thang
That our skin's coated in the hue of earth.

Once Upon a Time

Once upon a time, there
Was a land of the free
And a home of the brave.
The land was built
Without the help of slaves.
The black man had it made,
Because the white man saved
Him from being depraved
By amending his niggerly ways.

Once upon a time, meritocracy reigned.
The black man was rewarded
For his hard work and unrestrained
By any form of societal chains.
The ghetto was rich in resources
And prospering black businesses.
It was a land flowing with milk and honey,
Where people had the means to make legal money.

Once upon a time is a fairytale
That we know all too well.
It fails to keep it real
About how we deal
With all this pain
And still maintain.

Once upon a time is bullshit,
Preached from the pulpit
Of passive-aggressive white supremacists
And our own masochistic, black Judases.
The Grimm reality is masked by a happy ending
That most people still believe in.

Frankenstein

Frankenstein
Has created a monster.
The African American
Is a product of a failed plan
To convert the African
Man to a European
In a foreign land.

Frankenstein
Has created a monster—
And that is himself—
Lavishing in wealth
While depleting black societal health
Through diabolical schemes of stealth.

Two monsters
Diametrically opposed—
One force of utter chaos,
Of which madness was bestowed;
One vessel of corruption, courting self-destruction,
Corrodes until it inevitably explodes.

This monstrous collision,
Fueled by the derision
Of one man by another.
Frankenstein will discover
That the monster
Is himself.
And his creation
Will slowly forsake him
To his death.

The American Dream

The American dream
Leeches on the nightmares
Of the black reality.
Destiny manifested,
Resulted in ghetto slums infested
With depravity and lack,
The perks of being black.

The American dream
Is a lullaby
That keeps us all pacified
By the propaganda
Of those with hidden agendas.
It's a scripted incentive
In need of no further addendums.

It

America calls me it every day.
The project walls howl it in my sleep.
My stomach roars it when I have none to eat.
The Jumpman mocks me with it, 'cause my life
Is less valuable than the shoes on my feet.

I laugh when I hear somebody offended by the word.
Am I the only one to whom it is never unheard?
Every brick that built this country cries out that I continue to serve,
And I even here whisperings of it between two little birds.
The body language of white Americans says it without uttering words,
And their unapologetic glances say it's what we deserve.

Ode to Columbia

Malcolm warned me about you.
You dug me for all my gold.
You made me feel like the man,
At the expense of my own soul.
You choreograph my destiny,
While you plunder all that I own.
You borrowed so much from me,
And still it is you that I owe.
I saw what you did to Martin;
You brought the end of his days.
You prostitute his name
And spit all over his grave.
For you I do everything,
And still constantly I slave.
You kill my innocent children
And pay me the minimum wage.
I thought I could change you,
But you're stuck in your ancient ways.

Harlem Nights

What happens to a slave deferred from freedom?

Do we need him?
Does he believe every lie
That we feed him?
How long can we deceive him?
How do we sleep at night
Knowing the nature of his plight?

Perhaps, it is more dangerous if he knows
Than if he doesn't know
That he lies so low
On the totem pole.
After all, the bottom is more
Pleasant than limbo—
But for us lies are more
Pleasant than truth told.

What happens to a lie deferred from truth?

Does it hold,
Even after it's centuries old?

Or does it explode?

YOUNG JOSEPH

Contradiction

The black man is a walking contradiction,
Supposed to smile through the bloodshed
And love the ways of those who cause his affliction—
Living in a flimsy facade, the nature of being European bred
And fed to the wolves of this Caucasian establishment.
His every ambition tore asunder,
When victory is defeat in this lose-lose situation.
True knowledge is unspeakable pain,
When you begin to grasp the insurmountable odds
That stand before you with no foreseeable gain.
To what world can you lay claim,
When you straddle between two opposite planes
Of existence, and death awaits any attempt to distance
Yourself from the black and the white?
Whose hand gets raised in a self-inflicting fight?
Knowing the obstacles that we face, we find delight
In the fact that we still choose to fight.
The battle scars of contradiction
Remind us that the black man is walking Sol Invictus.

Lifeless Eyes

Lifeless eyes
I despise
Watching black lives
Zombified
A legion of
Black youth
With no room
For improvement
Cooks
And grocery sales clerks
Catching the bus
And rail to work.
I'm alert
To this frequent
Occurrence
Of the same sources
Of employment
Of those of dark pigment.
There's lint on my company
Shirt, but I'm so focused on the hurt.
Those of my shared skin,
I admire the work they put in.
But to what end?
It's them that I avenge
And extend
A helping hand to.

Ghetto-Born Dreams

Most ghetto-born dreams
Die prematurely.
A day
Ago
A young adolescent
Died in a dream team jersey,
An embryonic Kobe
Lost too early.
That
Same day
His homies
Gave up hoping
That
Thoughts
Would become things
When they dreamed,
'Cause tragedy
Cremated their seeds of prosperity.
A bloody smear in the mirror of young prepubescents
As they remain below the heavens,
'Cause it becomes evident that they may
Never reach the skies.
And if they had nine lives
In the hood, they could die nine times
Times nine.
Salvation becomes crime.
Dreams become lies.
Society they despise.
Most ghetto-born dreams
Drift too far away from reality.

Sound of the Dead Body

If a body falls in the ghetto,
Does it make a sound?
Did America hear the rounds
When they gunned him down?
While the average person peacefully sleeps,
His ghetto kinfolk mourn and weep.
His giant heart no longer beats.
The Jumpman grounded on his feet.
The murder rate he couldn't beat.
He died before he reached his peak,
Thinking that he let his family down.
This young man who was college bound
Is now deprived of the chance
To make them proud.
The rest of the country had him on mute
And didn't hear the killer shoot.
His story won't make the national news,
Another victim of the boys in blue.
This tragic story is sad but true.
Imagine the pain if it were you.

Bounty

There's a bounty on the head
Of a black man with dreads.
There's a large sum of money
For shooting someone with a hoodie.
There's an active hit list
For black men playing loud music.
There's a dollar for each slug
Aimed at a black youth on drugs.
There are free life sentences
For each troubled youth convicted.
There's a certain black targeted
By a silhouette marksman.
There's a license to do rotten
To those misguided and forgotten.
There's no harm in shots
Fired at the tadpoles of the projects.
Stainless-steel pistols
Don't second-guess whether
To sever young, tethered souls,
Whose lives will never unfold.
It's legal to aim and squeeze
At Young Thugs and Chief Keefs.
There's no love for a thug
And no sympathy for a nigga
Until the whole black world
Finds out a white man pulled the trigger.
There's no hesitation to shoot them,
Because they fit the description.
These black zombies are dismissed
Like *Call of Duty* victims.

Bounty hunters thrive in this system,

And Xbox isn't the system.

The usual suspects

Are a collection of black derelicts.

In the police lineup,

An upstanding black man identified them.

The ones whom black leaders wish would disappear

Are the ones most likely to not see another year.

The ones that "set black folks years back"

Are the ones easily smeared from existence.

It's open season on miscreants,

And from the shadows come black militants,

Appalled that white murderers get slapped on the wrist.

We should have seen this coming

When we provided the police sketch.

The ones whom we neglect

Are the ones unprotected.

There's an outline in chalk

For a generation lost.

There's blood on the hands

Of a finger-pointing black man,

Because when they were given the chance,

They testified on the stand.

This stereotypical horde

Is guilty of crime at large

And sentenced to a lifetime

Of hate-based violence.

Young black outlaws—

Pigeonholed on the gallows.

When it's too late, we riot,

Because it's too hard to digest.

The obligatory protest

And then back to our regularly scheduled programs.

If you shed real tears,
Then hold black pariahs dear.
Don't make any black
Man an outcast,
Because the one cast out
Meets the handgun's mouth.
And they'll keep kissing death
Until there ain't none left.
They're itching to murder
A young Nat Turner.
The murderers think that they're doing us a favor.
That's one less thug who met his maker.
That's one less gangster
And one less troublemaker.
That's one less nuisance
That you don't have to deal with.
That's America's solution
To the black community's pollution.
If we weren't so stupid,
We wouldn't have to lose them.
It's sad that we went
And put targets on their backs.
They eradicate the blacks
Whom our leaders don't respect.
It is easy to kill
Someone no one will miss.
But when reality hits,
We just clench our fists.
We were dreaming about progress
And woke up in a cold sweat.
There's no time for rest;
The nightmare persists.
One more red strike off the hit list,

And another violent murder of no consequence.
We should keep our arms open
For our prodigal sons.
There's nothing that can be done
Once they're gone.

Joseph

My brothers gave my life away.
They threw me into the cistern
And then sold me into slavery
And hoped that I'd never return.

My brothers let me go astray
And wouldn't guide me back.
My brothers made me castaway;
Their support is what I lack.

My brothers left me stranded
And hopeless on a deserted island.
If I traveled the waters deep
In hopes that I would find them,
The bloodthirsty sharks would feast on me.
I'm leashed upon this island.

My brothers gave my life away,
And I'm lost up until this day.
In the face of all this negligence,
I may still rise to prominence.

Three-Fifths Compromise

Worthless scum—
The crumb of the black man.
He wishes he had a hand
In his own fate,
But options are slim
For those who have had their futures raped.
He's the only thing left
On America's plate—
That leftover food scraped
To the edge that Liberty doesn't want to taste.
He is regarded as a waste,
The milk spoiled past its date.
He's the excess fat
Left on the bone.
And when no one's looking, he's trashed,
Because that's where he belongs.
But he is not alone;
There are many of his kind
Who have long been disposed.
When you're less than a man,
And even less than a black man,
There's no reason to stand.
When you're not a part of the grand
Blueprint, you scheme
Outside of the lines,
Survival by any means.
The 60 percent man
Is a ghost in this land,
A long-dead apparition
Whose life is superstition.

For him to be alive
Is fiction in the eyes
Of the minds
That tossed him by the wayside.
Three-fifths of a man
Is not quite a man.
And if you're not a quite a man,
Your life is not worth a damn
To any passive oppressor
Considered to be two-fifths greater.

ESPN

The worldwide leader—
In chattel breeding.
The worldwide minstrel—
Blackface replaced by field goals.
They will publicize you
And then criticize you.
On their backs, black
Slaves built a nation.
On their backs, black
Athletes fund PWInstitutions.
They love you when you're winning
And crack the whip when you're losing.
You're only human
When you entertain.
They pull all the strings,
But they look for you to blame.
And the moment your performance suffers,
They auction you off to the highest bidder.
The worldwide leader's a coliseum
That really should be a mausoleum,
Where gladiators bleed themselves to near death
And end their careers with nothing left.

The worldwide leader
Is the hoodwide Bible
That niggas watch
For their recital
Of all the thoughts
That it tells you to think
And all the truth
That it makes you believe.

Like: "This slave
Is better than that slave,
Because this slave
Gets us paid."
Sportscenter
Became their mentor.
My brothers abandoned all other ways
For the life of a slave who entertains.
They give them their everything
For a fraction of a chance to entertain—
Thrice as many people with a billion made
As players who are in the NBA.
Team owners twiddle their thumbs
While a player diligently dribbles a ball like a drum.
They held you up like you were "the one"
And martyred you when your prime was done.
You traded your more valuable intellect
To be the most valuable puppet.
Meanwhile, the audience has succumbed to bloodlust,
As they watch the bodies fall with a resounding thud—
Good people reduced to savages,
With no empathy for those held captive.
On cue, here comes the applause sign,
And their hands follow right behind.
"DaDaDa DaDaDa."

TEARS

Trail of Tears

Four hundred years of tears
Form rivers
That have flowed
Through every slum,
Baptizing the projects
In blood.

The soil of the hood became mud,
Making it natural
For every resident to do dirt.
Ancient and dusky
Those rivers must be.
Those tears will never dry.
They're as wet as when
They dripped from a tortured eye,
The only remnant of a silent cry.

I've known rivers:
Rivers that drown my brothers
Every day,
Rivers with currents too bold
For young children to play,
Rivers with floating corpses
Of grandmothers who prayed.

I've known rivers,
And they've known me.
They've become well acquainted
With my feet,
Because I walk above them
With ease.

I followed the trail of tears
To where I needed to be.
My journey over the years
Has qualified me to lead.

Shards

This mirror that I stare into,
Broken shards
I always knew.

I piece them back together,
Hoping
It isn't true.

I cut my hands
Every time,
Trying to make it whole.

I close my eyes,
Make up lies,
And run from what I know.

Broken shards
Of glass
Will never be the same again.

Broken shards
Of glass
Remain broken until the end.

Caged Lion

My friends are dying…
My family is struggling…
My eyes are crying…
These times are trying,
But it can't be—
Caged lion to be set free.

Star X

A pair of star-cross'd lovers take their lives.
This is the end when my two worlds collide;
When one lives, the other dies.

One foot in each costs a hefty price.
Patrons of both court suicide.
A pair of star-cross'd lovers take their lives.

I fooled myself not once, but twice.
I don't belong on either side;
When one lives, the other dies.

Night slays day, and days slays night—
Two foes, with each of whom I'm allied.
A pair of star-cross'd lovers take their lives.

One self-destructive, fatal fight—
Two jagged blades, a single knife.
When one lives, the other dies.

Far too late to make it right!
Far too late to change the tide!
A pair of star-cross'd lovers take their lives;
When one lives, the other dies.

Expatriate

Red blood,
Blue hearts,
And dying stars ablaze…

Black faces
Left speechless,
Bleeding away the days…

It's like I live in another country
From
The red,
The white, and
The blue.

It's like my world is far away
From
Liberty,
Justice, and
Truth.

My soul bleeds red,
My heart turns blue,
And my star is fading away.

I drown in blood;
I breathe in pain
On every gloomy day.

The stars;
The stripes;
The red, blue, and white
Were never mine to claim.

Black,
Red, blue, and white
Don't mix.
America lacks a conscience.

Bodies as Currency

Bodies as currency
And sex for trade.
It is a horror to see
This twisted chess game
In which dollars become human collars
And living flesh is the object of barter.
In this game, human beings are pawns,
And there is no honor among kings—
Treacherous imposters, for kings they are not,
With their foul schemes and plots.
There is no honor among scum,
For that is what they've become—
Pawns in a much bigger game,
For manipulating the defenseless and young.
In this exchange of human bodies,
Human trafficking is more akin to human tragedy—
The error of indecent souls succumbed to fallacy,
Doomed to imprisonment in their own moral dungeon,
Victims of self-inflicted judgment,
With no need to plunge them
Into the depths of their own guilt,
As they pay the debt for the dirty empire that they've built—
Debt that will never heal the wounds of the lives that they've crippled,
Lives that long to resuscitate their dreams long slain.
They exchange bodies as currency, but there is no bargain for pain.

Newfound Revelation

Newfound revelation,
Accompanied by a stinging sensation—
The realization
That things
Are not at all what they seem
Can bring a man to his knees
And squeeze
The inner membranes
Of his mind.

Insane,
Mental suicide
Arrives when you find
What you never intended to find.
What you held to be divine,
All lies
That led to deicide.

Those with clear eyes,
Twenty-twenty, terrified
By what they see
That others can't.

It's hard to see the truth
And hold your stance.
It's hard to see the noose
Around your neck.
It's hard to know the youth
You can't protect.
It's hard to know that you
Can't pave the way.

It's hard to know that you
Can't afford to dig a grave.
Newfound cremation.

The Underworld

I've emerged from the underworld and
Still hear their pleas.
I've watched it crumble in nature's hand.

I've seen its worst, yet still I stand.
It's left so many down on their knees,
[But] I've emerged from the underworld and

I mourn the land.
I've muted its screams.
I've watched it crumble in nature's hand.

I've morphed into a man
From an overlooked weed.
I've emerged from the underworld and

Its language I understand.
I've felt it bleed.
I've watched it crumble in nature's hand.

I've earned my tan
In its sweltering heat.
I've emerged from the underworld and
I've watched it crumble in nature's hand.

WAKANDA

Wakanda

All that remains of Wakanda
Are ash and rubble,
Remnants of the struggle.
Necropolis remains—
The golden city has crumbled.
Wakanda is gone—
So long
To the ebony empire.

All that remains of Wakanda
Is a queen's dying scream,
A shriek of pure emotion
Evoked from a dream destroyed
And archives of culture incinerated.
A once mighty nation obliterated
Into fragments
And scattered across
The globe,
With memories of
Brighter days
Imprisoned in the
Vibranium exoskeletons
Of our fiery hearts.

All that remains of Wakanda
Are her bastard sons,
Cheap imitations
Of the true manifestation
Of their bloodline.
Wakanda still has hope
For what her sons
Could be.

All that remains of Wakanda
Cannot be preserved
For much longer.
The queen's screams
Can only reach
Our ears for so long.

All that remains of Wakanda
Are ash and rubble,
Remnants of the struggle.
Necropolis remains—
The golden city has crumbled.
Wakanda is gone—
So long
To the ebony empire.

Black Artifacts

All I see is a collection of black artifacts,
Remnants of the ancient world not left intact.
The shreds of ancestry have severed their ties.
In divorce, the former bride and groom each unknowingly die.
My, my, how time flies!
How comfortable we've become within our disguise.
European and African both we despise—
Entangled within a web of lies.
Diaspora, diaspora, the tale of infinite horrors—
Stripped of our very essence as apples without their core.
Before we can look forward to what the future has in store,
We must remember and reflect upon the past that is no more.
These broken pieces of culture may never be fully restored,
So we can only grasp fragments of our forgotten ancestral lore.

Scramble for Africa

Little do they know
That the true gold
Is the African soul.
And that all the African valuables
That they laud, extol,
And subjugate under their control
Are glittering examples of fool's gold.

Black Royalty

The one who wears the crown
Cannot be held down.
The one who sits atop the throne
Does not walk alone.
Black kings are unfazed
By dark days.
Black queens can freeze
Time with a dark gaze.
Black royalty, authority,
And sovereignty
Crush the plagues of poverty
With bloodstained blades of equality.
Black conquests and voyages
In the name of our lineage of royalty,
Black Midases spread gold,
As all the paths they stroll
Turn to yellow-brick roads,
To and from their castle abodes.
Black queens and kings galore
With infinite room for more
To conquer and explore,
I request and implore.
Black kings and queens
Are what I dream.
So when I lay to sleep,
Instead of sheep
I count black kings and queens,
And over mountains they leap.

CHECKMATE

Pawns

Pawns…
Black pawns
Standing on
The front line
From A7 to H7,
Inching one step
At a time to our deaths.
Black pawns stepping
Forward till there ain't none left.
Ain't no lookin' back—
Ain't no do-overs or switching
To white pieces from black.
Possessors of the
Least means of attack,
But maybe, just maybe,
We overcome the power that we lack.
After all, unsuspecting black pawns together
Can check a white king in his tracks.

Hills

We build hills—
Hills of doubt,
Hills of clout,
Hills of things we can't live without.

We build hills—
Hills of good,
Hills of bad,
Hills between happy and sad.

We build hills—
Hills of invincibility,
Hills of stability,
Hills of integrity.

We build hills—
Hills of nothingness,
Hills of stress,
Hills that are ultimately worthless.

We build hills—
Hills that limit us,
Hills that kill us,
Hills that in the wrong direction steer us.

Ants build hills.
Humans build will—
The will for the future,
The will to make success a part of your nature,
The will to push past all the pain and torture,
The will that eventually brings about good fortune.

Thoreau stated that there was much more to life
Than industrious work devoid of life.
For ants build hills industriously,
And what separates them from us, if we
Toil away industriously
Toward tasks bereft of meaning?

If we built will,
Instead of hills,
Our dreams
Would heal our broken wings.
And Langston Hughes would smile again,
Knowing the will
That he had built
Leapt from the page
And gave us wealth.

Wealth of knowledge to build more will
And curse the ants that build those hills—
Hills that cripple who we really are,
Hills that eclipse the light of shining stars,
Hills that we've allowed to go too far—
And suppress the will that makes us more,
More than ants without a cause,
Willing to do the bidding of our thoughts
Rather than be forbidden to take shots.
A life building hills is a life lost,
And losing yourself is an unworthy cost.

For ants get stepped on every day,
But they don't regret that they never played.
While most humans slave and slave and slave
And lose their lives with no ways paved.

What difference exists between ants and them,
If they've both built hills for days and days?
Trapped inside an endless maze
Of repetition and dismay,
They've buried themselves in the works of others.
But for works of their own, they've never bothered
To give them time,
To make them fine,
And dig for gold within,
Their own mines (minds).
An ant hill toppled was a waste of time,
But monuments of will are hard to unbind.
Strong human will is an infinite flame
That the sands of time can't even tame.

The will that we build lights the way
For bearers of torch in future days.
The will of the legends never went away;
They pervade our thoughts every day,
Anxious to wash our hills away,
Until one day that they break loose
And save our necks from conformity's noose.
On a day like that this ant deduced
That "I am human" and embraced the truth.

Levitate

Impossible for an outsider to relate
To the unfortunate twists of fate
That riddle my current climate.
The dream being nothing but a subconscious escape.
The cake being nothing but a tease, just a taste
Of the constructive destruction that lies in my wake.
I dare not take more time to contemplate!
I stand, I climb, I rise, I leap, I levitate!

Matt Murdock

Destiny smiles upon
The man without fear,
The man of whom doubt
Never lingers upon the tips of his ears
And is never weighed down
By the limitations of yesteryear.

Destiny smiles upon
The daredevil,
The insane thrill seeker,
And status-quo rebel,
The man incessant on
Taking life to another level.

Destiny smiles upon
The hero,
The man who courageously
Leads where few can follow;
The person whose
Level of cowardice is zero.

Destiny smiles upon
The defense and the prosecution,
The man that makes a compelling argument
For himself with his actions,
And then stands firmly in favor
Of his beliefs and own volition.

Destiny smiles upon
Matt Murdock,
The man whose curious nature

Frees him from the spell of the flock
And urges him to pursue life
With the methodology of Sherlock.

Pipe Dreams

Dreams drained down the pipe
And sleepless nights,
Countless rounds lost via harsh decisions,
Bouts that test the extremes of vigilance,
Clinging dearly to life's antithesis,
The onset of the symptoms of loneliness,
No answer for the hooks and jabs of your opponent—
These are man's defining moments.
Dancing on the devil's doorstep,
In memory of those for whom you once wept,
You'd have taken an L if you had on opportunity slept.
The light often flickers brilliantly on the brink of death,
One final stand turned into a firm step—
To the plate with an audacious left,
Hook, jab, uppercut, and off its feet adversity is swept.

Midas Mindset

Midas mindset—everything he touches turns to gold.

Modern masterpiece—oh what a sight to behold!

Deep within the Trojan horse of him, there lies his soul,

The mythos of a man whose story has yet to be told.

A man possessed with a fervor that shackles couldn't hold

Steps into this brave new world to go forth and be bold.

Each day he writes a page of a story untold,

Refusing to give in to doubt and under the weight of the pressure fold.

His fate, to be great, that he already knows.

HOME

The Souls of Black Folk

The souls of black folk
Echoed through her throat,
And her vocals
Produced a note
That the audience couldn't resist,
Because it grabbed them by the
Ears and said: "Here,
Pay attention to this
Rich oral tradition,
Passed down from generations,
The voice of the black nation."

The souls of black folk
Sent chills down his spine,
As he spoke the gospel of the divine
And down from the pulpit he climbed
To preach the epistles of Simon
Peter to his congregation, eager
To feel the Word
Purge them of the earth
And remove all the hurt
By giving them new birth.

The souls of black folk
Course through my veins,
As I recite each line,
Sharing my mind
With those of my own kind.
My bondage, my freedom
Are what I need you to feel,
And through our

Voices we spill
Blood from once-concealed
Scabs that the discovery
Of the skeletons
In the closet of history
Prevent from fully healing.

The souls of black folk
Spoke to me
And wrote for me.
I'm in harmony
With every black
Voice that ever sang
And every black orator
That ever claimed
To be a vessel of
Black beauty.

When I speak,
The voices of black
Fieldsmen reach
The eardrums
Of their off-sprung
Children of the present.
Their message:
"Learn from our essence,
Because from our judgment
Your generation
Is the new black testament
Of ebony achievement,
Spawned and seeded
From the original continent."

Indeed, it's a new era
For the gray chimera.
Our lives are a sphinx riddle;
The wrong answer is fatal.
The riddle is as follows:
What's black and
White and red all over?
Does anyone know the answer?
It's the black man in the
White world, bled to death
From centuries of torture.
Africa is married to Europe,
And it's impossible to divorce
Her. The souls of black folk
Cry out for hope,
And the tears that they shed
Keep us afloat
While we choke
From the stranglehold
Of white hands on our throats.
Those same souls spoke
To me and passed the torch
Of our culture.
My generation will
Push black folk forward!

Footstep Blues

On a grossly neglected street,
Marching to his own imaginary beat,
I watched a Negro plant his feet.
Each step gave a glimpse
Of the paths he had tread.
His walk was a language
That I had read,
And few could understand
What it actually said.

I heard the horns
Of his gangsta bounce.
The sound of his kicks
On pavement drowned
Every other sound out.

Meanwhile, my walk
Danced to a slightly different beat.
Our signature styles
Collided on that jagged street.
In the midst of our percussive
Street melodies,
We nodded our heads
To acknowledge each other
As young black kindred.
Understood without being said,
Our music linked our telepathic threads.

Boogie-woogie
Bebop!
We grooved

And beat hopped
To street-feet hip-hop.

We spoke through footstep blues
And dope Nike shoes.
Footstep blues
And dope Nike shoes…
Footstep blues,
Jordan twos,
Gamma blues,
Ella Fitzgerald,
Satchmo Lou,
Langston Hughes…
Those footstep blues.

Home

I'm at home among those
Of my own skin tone.
When I'm connected to the
African subconscious, I'm never alone.
There's no clone for the instinctive
Bravado of the sons of the Congo jungle.

I'm at home among streetball
And barbershop small talk.
When I step on the playground courts
Where black legends once walked,
I feel their presence
On surveillance like a hawk.

I'm at home among my kinfolk.
When family gets together,
It reminds me
Of a bond that can never be severed.
Transient moments shared with them
Are ingrained in my brain forever.

I'm at home among James Baldwin
And the wide-eyed dreams of Langston
Hughes, my hero—
And I never had the chance to thank him,
So I put my feet in the
Oversized shoes that he left,
And I stumbled when I stepped,
But at it I kept.

I'm at home in my own skin
And proud to be the heir
In a long line of black men.
I'm proud of my tan,
Knowing that it
Gets no better than a black man.

MUTABLE
CLOUD

Mutable Cloud

It is but a mutable cloud
That is always and never the same.
The nature of nature is shrouded
By our artificial campaigns.

Nature is an armillary sphere
Of components both here
And there, both near
To another snapshot in time,
As well as orbiting in a distant plane.

It is fundamentally unchanged,
And yet internally rearranged.
The nature of nature
Is foreign to our brains.

Nature is what it has been
From the beginning,
Yet every moment in time
Will never be experienced again.
Its rings keep spinning
In different ways,
But that sphere's still moving
At a constant speed.

It is both predictable
And unpredictable.
The nature of nature
Is an unsolvable riddle,
Of which the solution
Is always and never the same.

Slipping Sand

I tried to grasp it
Before my time ended.
Sand slipped through my finger,
Killing my desire to linger.
What do you do when
Your glass runs out of sand?
Me? I search for another glass,
Knowing that it won't last.
We move from glass
To glass,
Inside of a much bigger glass—
Glasses inside of a glass.
Flashes
Of brilliance pass,
Lasting
Until the last
Drip of sand,
Waning until the end.

Escher's Relativity

Sane is Insane

And Insane is Sane

For who could be Sane

While conscious of the chains

That make the world hang itself

That make the world hang itself

While conscious of the chains

For who could be Sane

And Insane is Sane

Sane is Insane

Temple

We live together, but we die alone.
We all inevitably inhabit the petrified forest
Of bodies turned to stone.
We shed our skin, our flesh, and our bone.
We all take that faithful step into the eerie unknown.

The body that was once a temple
Will eventually become a ruin,
An ancient, decaying carcass
For others to trample on.
What once was sacred will no longer be preserved.

The thoughts that were never acted upon,
Doomed to never be heard…
The ideas never manifested, lost…
And every regret eternally submerged
Into the grave, food for the vultures,
Those merciless scavenging birds.

We live together, but few of us ever
Stray away from the herd.
And when most of us die,
There isn't much to remember.
Yea, your body was your temple,
But will you ever leave a ripple,
Or was your life ordinary, mundane, and simple?
Those are the questions that people con temple,
Or rather contemplate too late,
As they put the definitive punctuation marks on your fate.
Did you ever do anything great?
Were you someone with whom others could relate?

Because your body is destined to dissipate,
But your body of work is capable of reaching an eternal, timeless state.

Your body of work is your temple,
Because it is the legacy that you leave behind.
And after you're long gone,
It is the only relic that people will find.
So unleash the shackles that enslave your mind
And embrace the path that your heart has defined.

Build your temple with intangible walls,
And they will be less likely to crumble and fall.
It is worth noting that those
Who were mentally strong
Were the people who lived
The most memorable lives of all.
Remember that no act is too small,
And no obstacle is too tall.

The residue that we leave on this earth
Is the stain that paints our temple walls,
And our greatest contributions create an ethereal mural.
Don't be afraid to walk before you crawl
Or be paralyzed by fear of your eventual stumble.
In life even when you're wrong and take a hard fall,
There is a good chance that you still made the right call.
So don't allow your misgivings to force you into a state of stall,
Because we all die, but most of us never truly live at all.

The Flow

The way that the pen marks the page one character at a time,
The sound produced from the drop of a dime,
The unexpected that looms and makes time a ticking landmine—
Those are the quintessential elements by which life is defined.

Separation exists not, and all things are combined,
But the poor human mind struggles to define.
We wrestle with the default and seek to categorize,
Foolish to the fact that all intertwines.
We flow against the current of the divine,
Unaware that blurring the lines
Enhances the visionary mind.

If we color the black-and-white
World, then we step outside the limitations of our mental confines.
Dance with the abstract and dine
With acts of eccentricity.

Live by the flow,
Go where it goes,
And know what it knows.

TREASURE

Treasure in the Wasteland

There is treasure in the wasteland,
Wealth mined from thriving in poor conditions,
And value from learning to walk in quicksand.

There are forsaken souls with a game plan,
An amethyst ambition to rise to a wealthy position.
There is treasure in the wasteland.

There is the wisdom of the cautionary tale of a battered man,
Gems gleaned from witnessing the hazards of moral attrition,
And value from learning to walk in quicksand.

There are turmoil and strife in the wasteland,
But the time spent between bottom dwellers is golden.
There is treasure in the wasteland.

There are scars and blisters on the hands
Of a silver-haired man, weathered from treasure huntin'
And [shaped by] value [gained] from learning to walk in quicksand.

Some who live there often wish for a better land,
But those who really pay attention
[Know that] there is treasure in the wasteland
And value from learning to walk in quicksand.

Metrorail Wisdom

Metrorail wisdom
From a corner store Confucius,
Living lucidly
Under the influence
Of cooked cocaine.
He exchanges
A wise saying
For loose change.

To find meaning
In what he's saying
Is to absolve
Him from the way
Society is portraying
His kind to be.
In their mind,
His mind
Should be
In a vegetative state,
But yet he relates
To life lessons that fate
Has allowed him to postulate
In good faith.

His experiences
Form the basis
And foundation
From which his wisdom
Hangs like the
Ancient gardens of Babylon.

Pearls

All women are pearls.

Power lies within the ability of a girl
To bring life into this world.

Strength is a single mother of two
Laboring to be a mother and a father too.

Peace is a grandmother's smile,
Still comforting you like when you were a child.

Trust is the bond that you and an older sister share;
It's the glue that makes you two an inseparable pair.

Love is the one woman with the keys to your soul,
The final puzzle piece that makes you whole.

A woman's hair is as precious as gold.
Her touch is soothing, never too hot nor too cold.
Her smell is the fragrance of nature's sweet perfume,
And her lips taste like apple nectar, fresh after bloom.

That mother of two
Could be a grandmother to you.
And your older sister who watched you as you grew
Could be a lover to someone of whom you have no clue.

Regardless of what they mean to you
And the great deeds that they've done for you,
All women are pearls,
Integral to this world.

Without a Woman

Without the sun,
There's no light.
Without eyes,
There's no sight.
Without a woman,
There's no life.
No light, no sight,
No day, no night.

Glaringly, it shows
That without a woman,
There are many noes,
Including a lonely Adam
With nowhere to go.
Without a woman,
Man corrodes,
Missing the rib
That makes him whole.

There are many things
That spark a man's soul,
But without a woman
They all lose their glow.
Sun don't shine,
Eyes don't show.
No brighter days,
No way to go.

Without a woman,
There's no life.
For a woman's worth,
There's no price.

Soul Deep

Beauty is only soul deep.
On true beauty we continually sleep.
I long for the woman
Who can make my soul fall apart
And then put it back together
Like it was from the start.
Beauty is in the words that she speaks.
Beauty is beyond her curves and physique.
I glanced at her thighs,
Mesmerized, and she told me
To "close [my] eyes
And come back to [her]
When [I] awake from [my] sleep,
Because beauty is only soul deep."

VACUUM

Vacuum

We're approaching a space
Devoid of matter—
Mindless chatter and nitpicks,
Collateral damage of critics.

We're approaching a place
Where meaning ends
And the reign of nonsense
Just begins.

We're approaching an abyss
Where individuality doesn't exist,
And life's intrinsic qualities
Are utterly diminished.

We're approaching the void
Where the greatest sound
Has become noise
That is canceled out
By the matterless
Condition of the crowd.

Within the vacuum
Positive vibration ceases,
And mental independence
Falls to pieces.

Padded Walls

Life, camera, action,
Within those padded walls!
The Hollywood *Truman*
Show knows no laws.
Come, witness the celebrities in their
Natural habitat, with all of their flaws!
Their compromised humanity
Has pushed them to the edge of insanity—
Watched by all and constantly attacked,
And then deemed psychotic
When they react to the straitjacket.
Bright, promising stars fall
When those white walls
Close in,
And their every action
Becomes a sin.
Celebrity mad men—
Lambasted when they've had enough
And the love that they're given is tough.
Within those padded walls, it's rough,
And soon there won't be enough
Wrong to satisfy our appetite
For gossip and mistrust.
We love when Achilles has a fragile heel,
So that we can completely ignore how he feels.
That's the celebrity life,
And for their every vice we lust.
The steep price of fame
Is to have your entire livelihood hanged
From the height of your grandest dreams.
The mission statement is simple:
"To entertain the people by any means
Unnecessary."

Masquerade Ball

Well played, well played!
You love me when need be
And hate me when I leave.
Up your sleeve
There are shapeshifting
Tricks—Shakespearean lit
Concealed by 50 Cent.
Realities of lust, envy, and pride
By tales of wise men frankincense, disguised.
Mimicries of celebrities whom you idolize
Hide the premature, unwatered seed inside.
Twitter fiction has transformed to addiction.
You've abandoned your prescription of real
To swallow delusions-of-grandeur pills.
Placebo infected you with falsehood—
Hallucinations of mafioso and bosshood—
Conclusions Gerber-fed to you
By ESPN; BET; and red, white, and blue.
You're some of everything,
But none of you.

And the owl questions us all,
As we dance and mingle at this ball.
All clamoring for the spotlight,
And under the bright lights,
Our flesh ignites—
White dwarfed by white lies.
We wanted to be stars,
And now here we are,
Struggling to hold on
Before being exposed

As black holes.
Social-media pseudonyms
Transformed us into holograms.
Our true selves, distant as a mirage,
Hidden beneath this daily facade.
Everyone is everyone else's slave.
Intense scrutiny awaits the brave.
Those with even a semblance of courage
Will soon find themselves betrayed.
Alas, we're living in this masquerade!
Well played, well played!